Rockin' Poppin'
Snare Drum

RHYTHM FUNDAMENTALS

Bart Robley

ISBN 978-1-57424-270-6
SAN 683-8022

Book Design by Roy David Dains at *Falcon Marketing Media*
www.FalconMarketingMedia.com

Copyright © 2011 CENTERSTREAM Publishing, LLC
P.O. Box 17878 - Anaheim Hills, CA 92817

www.centerstream-usa.com

Acknowledgments

My sincere thanks to the following people: my wife, Leah, for her constant support; the best musicians in the world: Sam Morrison, Steve Cenker (E.T. #1), Greg Kasparian (my Thunder Brother), Doreen Novotny, Mandy Burke, David Kurtz, Karl Sanger (thanks for everything!), Roy Dains and Mike Chiaravalloti; Justin Novotny; Dana Kasparian; Cyndi Morrison; Trey and Wendy Solberg; Michael Vail Blum at Titan Recording; Ron Middlebrook at Centerstream Publishing; everyone at Hal Leonard; Mark and Jacque Davies; Ken Hobson at Triskelion Events; Roy Burns, Ron Marquez, Chris Brady, Gabe Diaz, Jamie Harris and everyone at Aquarian Drumheads; Kim Graham, John Palmer, Brent Barnett, and everyone at Gretsch Drums and Gibraltar Hardware; Mike Dorfman and everyone at Trick Drums; Michael Vosbein and Kevin Vosbein at Bosphorus Cymbals; Bryan Scheidecker and Neil Larrivee at Vic Firth; Mark at Drum Star Wear; Gregg Bissonette; Ralph Humphrey; Tony Pia; Dom Famularo; Mo and Roger Palmateer; all of my drum students past and present; and to all the Sam Morrison Band fans who have stuck by us for so many years - thank you all from the bottom of my heart!

Introduction

When learning to play the drums or any musical instrument, the first thing you have to remember is to be patient with yourself. You are not in a hurry and you don't want to develop bad habits along the way. I encourage you to find a private instructor who can convey his or her thoughts to you in a clear and precise manner and eliminate the guess work.

I also believe it is imperative to learn how to read music. This book is a great way to get started down the right track to reading rhythm, rests and rolls. Be patient, take your time, and most of all, HAVE FUN!

HAPPY DRUMMING!

Bart Robley

The Following Rudiments are Re-Printed Courtesy of the Percussive Arts Society

PERCUSSIVE ARTS SOCIETY INTERNATIONAL DRUM RUDIMENTS

ALL RUDIMENTS SHOULD BE PRACTICED: OPEN (SLOW) TO CLOSE (FAST) TO OPEN (SLOW) AND/OR AT AN EVEN MODERATE MARCH TEMPO.

I. ROLL RUDIMENTS

A. SINGLE STROKE ROLL RUDIMENTS

1. SINGLE STROKE ROLL *

R L R L R L R L

2. SINGLE STROKE FOUR

R L R L   R L R L
L R L R   L R L R

3. SINGLE STROKE SEVEN

R L R L R L R
L R L R L R L

B. MULTIPLE BOUNCE ROLL RUDIMENTS

4. MULTIPLE BOUNCE ROLL

5. TRIPLE STROKE ROLL
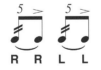
R R R L L L R R R L L L

C. DOUBLE STROKE OPEN ROLL RUDIMENTS

6. DOUBLE STROKE OPEN ROLL *
R R L L R R L L

7. FIVE STROKE ROLL *
R R L L

8. SIX STROKE ROLL
R   L R   L
L   R L   R

9. SEVEN STROKE ROLL *
R   L R   L
L   R L   R

10. NINE STROKE ROLL *
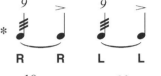
R   R   L   L

11. TEN STROKE ROLL *

R   R L   R   R L
L   L R   L   L R

12. ELEVEN STROKE ROLL *
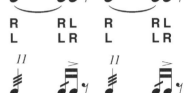
R   R L   R   R L
L   L R   L   L R

13. THIRTEEN STROKE ROLL *

R   R L   L

14. FIFTEEN STROKE ROLL *

R   L R   L R
L   R L   R

15. SEVENTEEN STROKE ROLL

R   R   L   L

II. DIDDLE RUDIMENTS

16. SINGLE PARADIDDLE *

R L R R L R L L

17. DOUBLE PARADIDDLE *

R L R L R R L R L R L L

18. TRIPLE PARADIDDLE

R L R L R L R R L R L R L R L L

19. SINGLE PARADIDDLE-DIDDLE

R L R R L L R L R R L L
L R L L R R L R L L R R

* These rudiments are also included in the original Standard 26 American Drum Rudiments.

PAS INTERNATIONAL DRUM RUDIMENTS page 2

III. FLAM RUDIMENTS

20. FLAM *

L R   R L

21. FLAM ACCENT *

L R   L   R   R L   R   L

22. FLAM TAP *

L R   R R L L   L R   R R L L

23. FLAMACUE *

L R   L   R   L R
R L   R   L   R R L

24. FLAM PARADIDDLE *

L R   L   R   R R L   R   L L

25. SINGLE FLAMMED MILL

L R   R   L   R R L   L   R L

26. FLAM PARADIDDLE-DIDDLE *

L R   L   R   R L L   L R   L   R L L R R

27. PATAFLAFLA

L R   L   R R L L   L R   L   R R L

28. SWISS ARMY TRIPLET

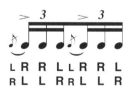

3   3

L R R   L L R R L
R L L   R R L L R

29. INVERTED FLAM TAP

L R   L R L   R L R   L R L   R

30. FLAM DRAG

L R   L   L R R L   R R L

IV. DRAG RUDIMENTS

31. DRAG *

L L R   R R L

32. SINGLE DRAG TAP *

L L R   L R R L   R

33. DOUBLE DRAG TAP *

L L R L L R   L R R L R R L   R

34. LESSON 25 *

L L R   L   R   L L R   L   R
R R L   R   L   R R L   R   L

35. SINGLE DRAGADIDDLE

R R L   R   R R L L R L L

36. DRAG PARADIDDLE #1 *

R L L R   L   R   R   L R R L   R   L L

37. DRAG PARADIDDLE #2 *

R L L R L L R   L   R R L   R R L   R R L   R L L

38. SINGLE RATAMACUE *

3   3

L L R   L R L   R R L   R L R

39. DOUBLE RATAMACUE *

3   3

L L R L L R   L R L   R R L   R R L   R L R

40. TRIPLE RATAMACUE *

3   3

L L R L L R L L R   L R L   R R L R R L R R L   R L R

FOR MORE INFORMATION ON BECOMING A MEMBER OF THE PERCUSSIVE ARTS SOCIETY CONTACT PAS AT:
110 W. WASHINGTON STREET, SUITE A, INDIANAPOLIS, IN 46204 • E-MAIL: percarts@pas.org WEB SITE: WWW.PAS.ORG

Table of Contents

Basic Quarter-Note Exercises

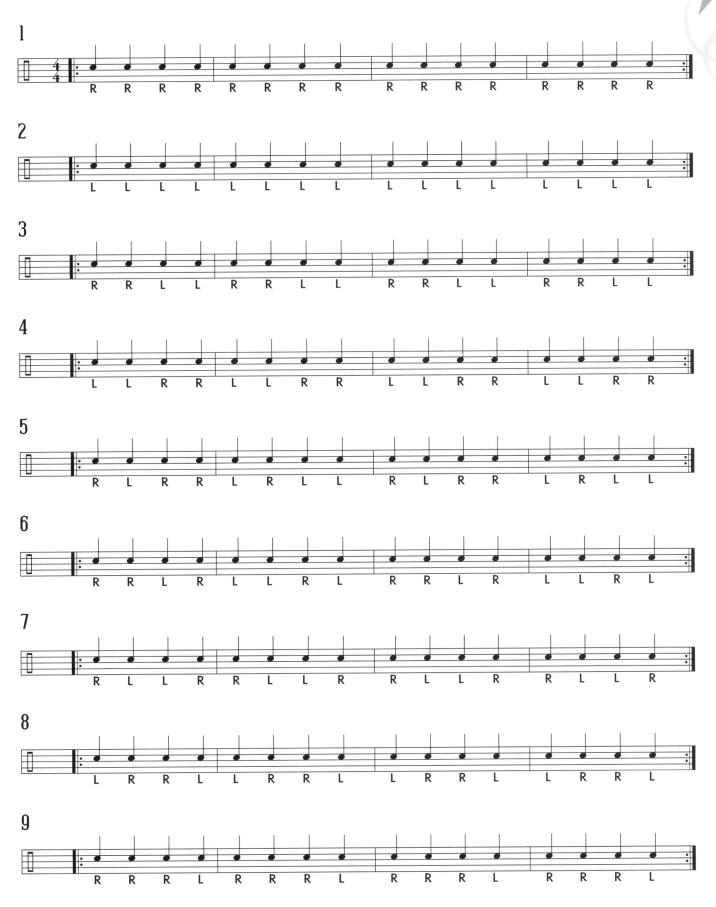

Basic Quarter-Note Exercises

10

L L L R L L L R L L L R L L L R

11

R R R L L L L R R R R L L L L R

12

L L L R R R R L L L L R R R R L

PHOTO: CYNDI MORRISON

Timing Exercises

Exercise 1

Exercise 2

Timing Exercises

Exercise in 3/4 ver. 1

CD TRACK 2

Exercise in 3/4 ver. 2

Quarter & Eighth Note Exercises

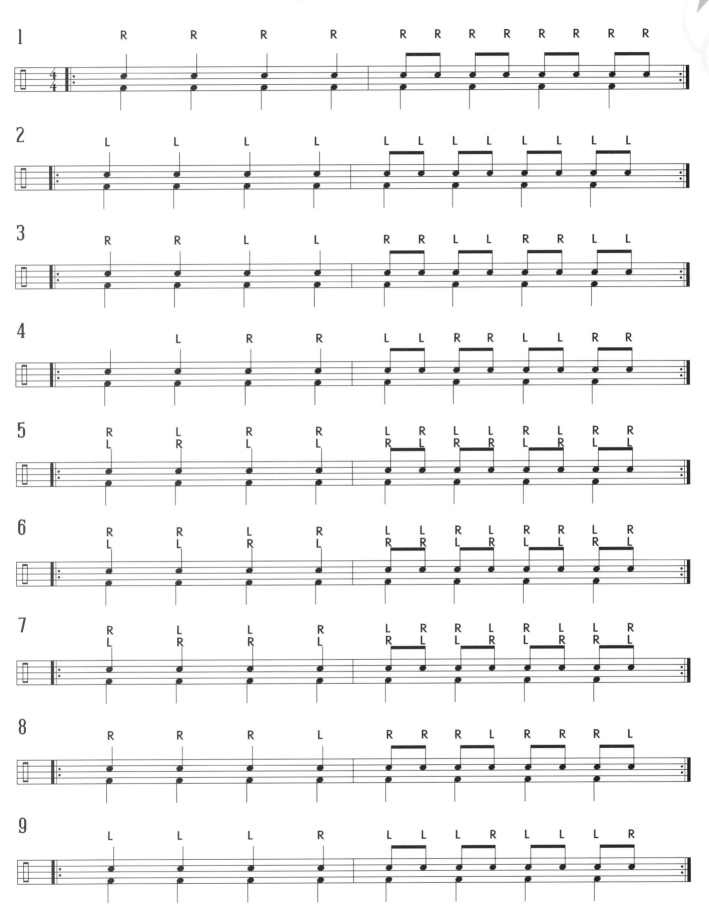

Quarter & Eighth Note Exercises

PHOTO: LEAH ROBLEY

Timing Exercises

Exercise 4

Timing Exercises

Exercise 5

Eighth Note Rest

Eighth Note Rest

Eighth Note Rest

Exercise 6

CD TRACK 5

Exercise 7

Eighth Note Rest

Exercise 8

CD TRACK 6

Rockin' Poppin' **1**
Snare Drum

Exercise 9

CD TRACK 7

Rockin' Poppin' 1
SnareDrum

Quarter & Sixteenth Note Combinations

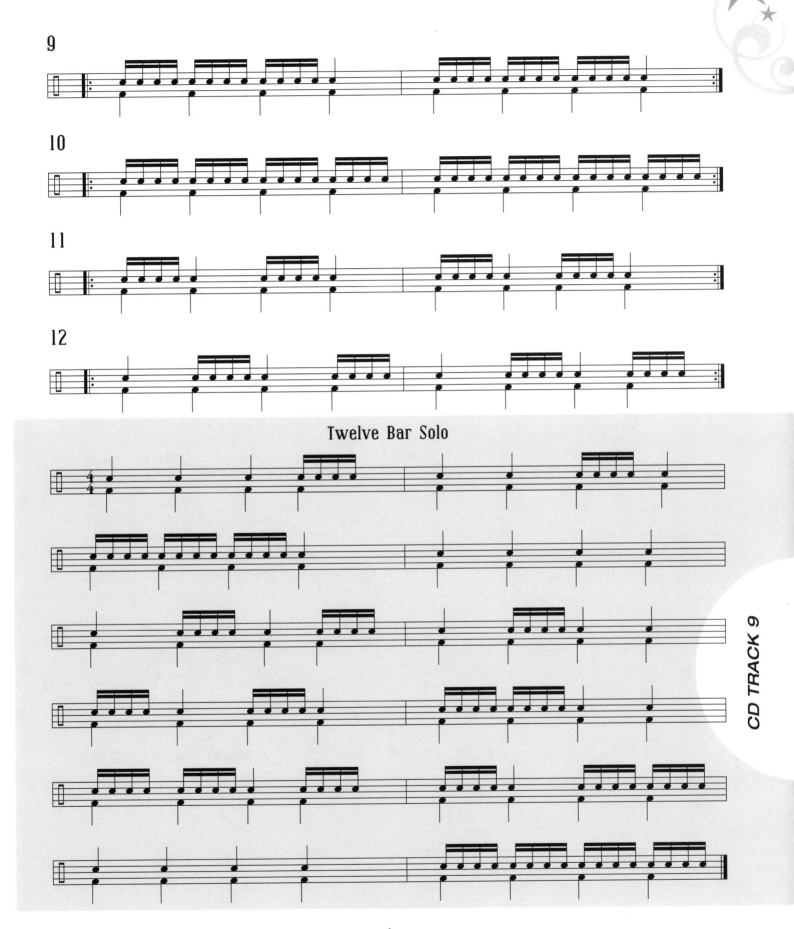

Twelve Bar Solo

CD TRACK 9

Eighth & Sixteenth Note Combinations

CD TRACK 10

Eighth & Sixteenth Note Combinations

10

11

12

Twelve Bar Solo

CD TRACK 11

Rockin' Poppin' **1**
Snare Drum

Eighth & Sixteenth Note Combinations

Thirty-Two Bar Solo

Eighth & Sixteenth Note Combinations

Thirty-Two Bar Solo (PT.2)

CD TRACK 12

Eighth & Sixteenth Note Combinations

E and -

Eighth & Sixteenth Note Combinations

E and -

10

11

12

Twelve Bar Solo

Rockin' Poppin' **1**
SnareDrum

Eighth & Sixteenth Note Combinations

Eighth & Sixteenth Note Combinations

And A -

10

11

12

Twelve Bar Solo

CD TRACK 16

Rockin' Poppin' 1

Snare Drum

Eighth & Sixteenth Note Combinations

E and A Combined

CD TRACK 17

Eighth & Sixteenth Note Combinations

E and A Combined

CD TRACK 18

Rockin' Poppin' 1
Snare Drum

Eighth & Sixteenth Note Combinations

E and A Combined

Eighth & Sixteenth Note Combinations

Thirty-Two Bar Solo

Thirty-Two Bar Solo (Pt.2)

CD TRACK 19

Rockin'
Poppin' **1**
Snare Drum

Eighth & Sixteenth Notes

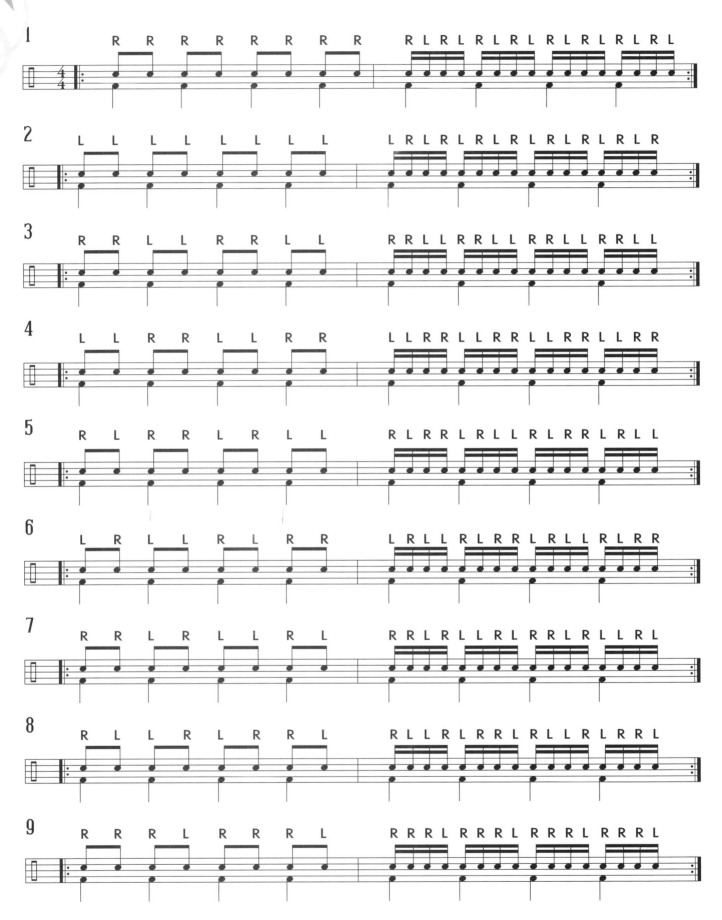

Eighth & Sixteenth Notes

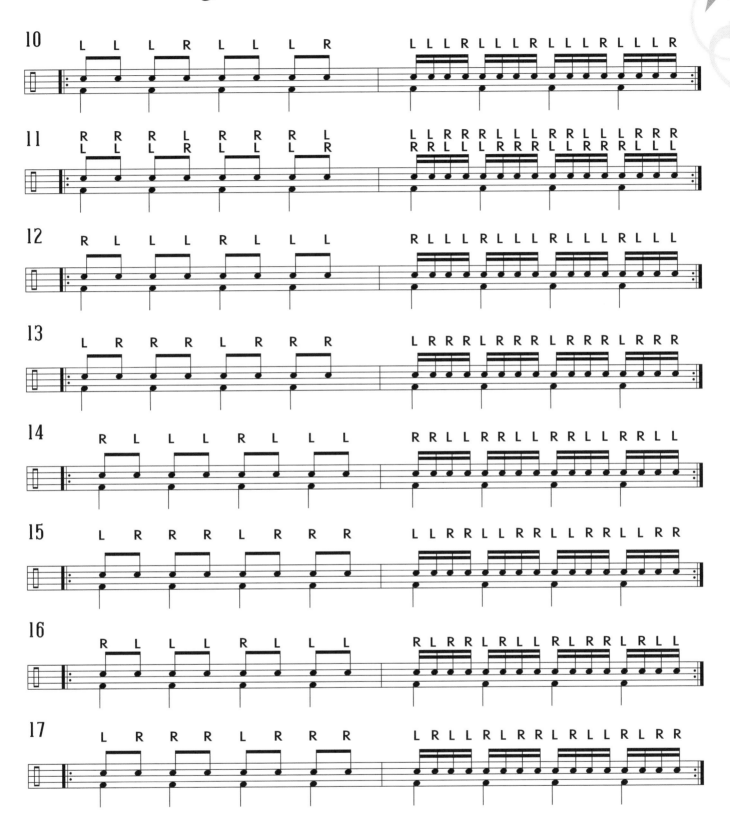

Rebound Strokes

Rebound Eighth Notes

A double-stroke roll is achieved when the drum stick rebounds off the drumhead, allowing it to only bounce two times. When learning how to do this, it is best to start by doubling Eighth Notes. Count the doubled Eighth Note as a Sixteenth Note. By the time you get to Exercise 12, you will have a controlled roll.

Rockin' Poppin' 1
Snare Drum

Rebound Sixteenth Notes

Once you have mastered doubling Eighth Notes, try doubling Sixteenth Notes, creating a Thirty-Second Note. This is the basis for all rudimental drum rolls.

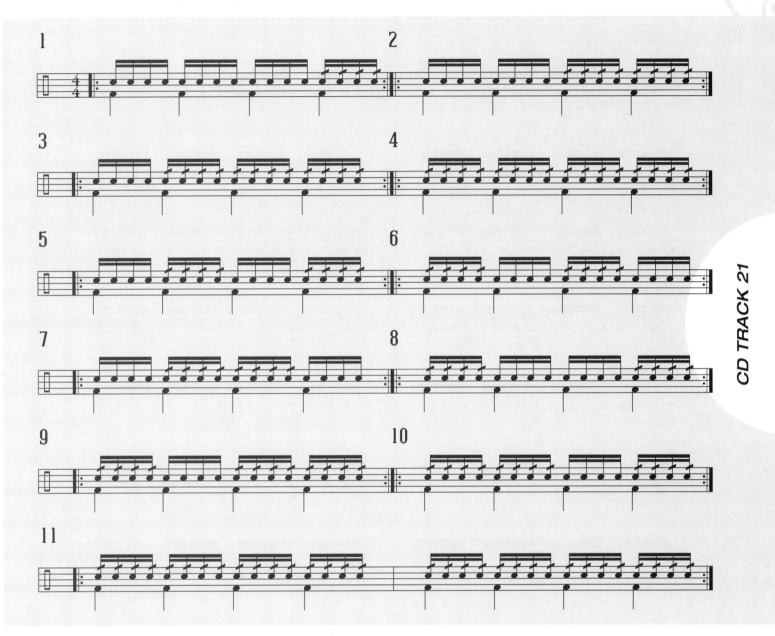

Sixteen Bar Solo

Rockin' Poppin' **1**
Snare Drum

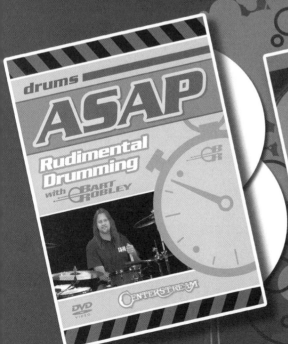

Developing 5 and 9 Stroke Rolls

All of our rudimental rolls are built using Thirty-Second Notes. We developed a Thirty-Second Note in the previous section by doubling a Sixteenth Note. Now we will work these into two rudimental rolls, the 5 and 9 stroke. To understand the 5 and 9 stroke rolls, start by doubling an Eighth Note and ending on the Quarter Note to achieve the correct number of strokes. Once you have built this into a smooth roll which sounds and feels musical, move onto doubling a Sixteenth Note. This will be the basis not only for the 5 and 9 stroke rolls, but for all of our rudimental rolls.

PHOTO: CYNDI MORRISON

Developing 5 and 9 Stroke Rolls

Developing a 5 Stroke Roll

CD TRACK 23

Developing a 9 Stroke Roll

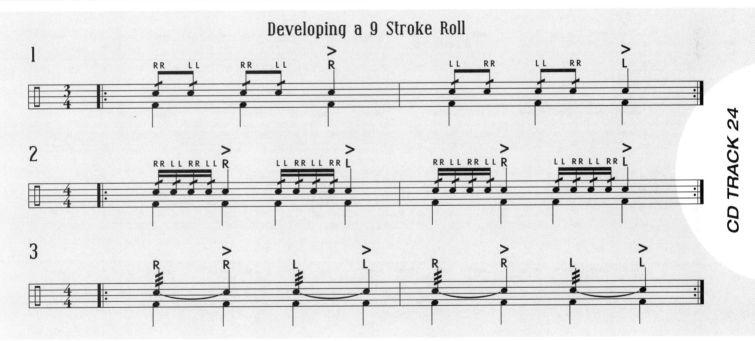

CD TRACK 24

Developing 5 and 9 Stroke Rolls

Thirty-Two Bar Solo Using 5-Stroke Rolls

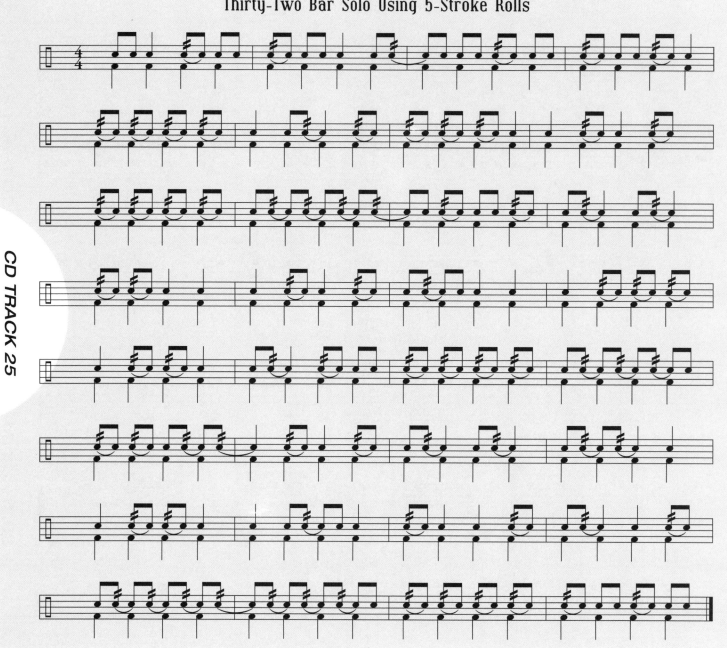

Developing 5 and 9 Stroke Rolls

Thirty-Two Bar Solo Using 9-Stroke Rolls

CD TRACK 26

Developing 5 and 9 Stroke Rolls

Thirty-Two Bar Solo Using 5 and 9 Stroke Rolls

CD TRACK 27

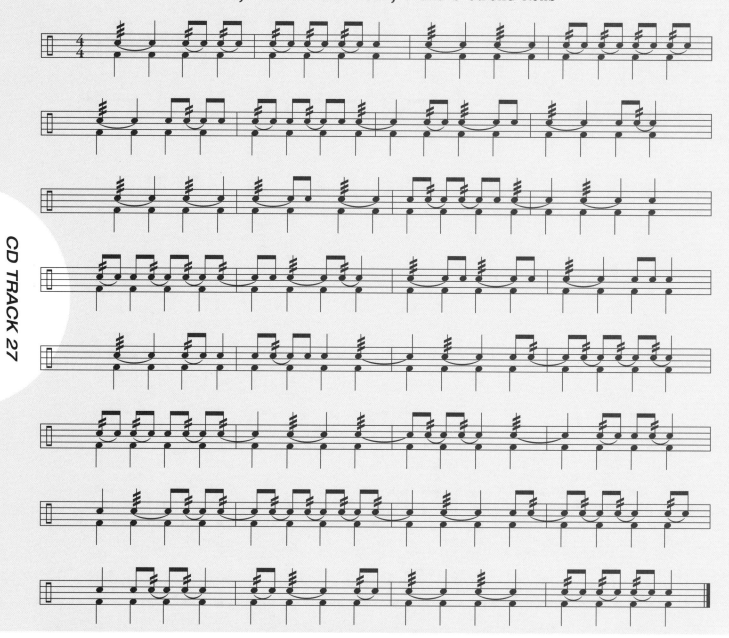

Rolled Eighth & Sixteenth Note Combinations

E and –

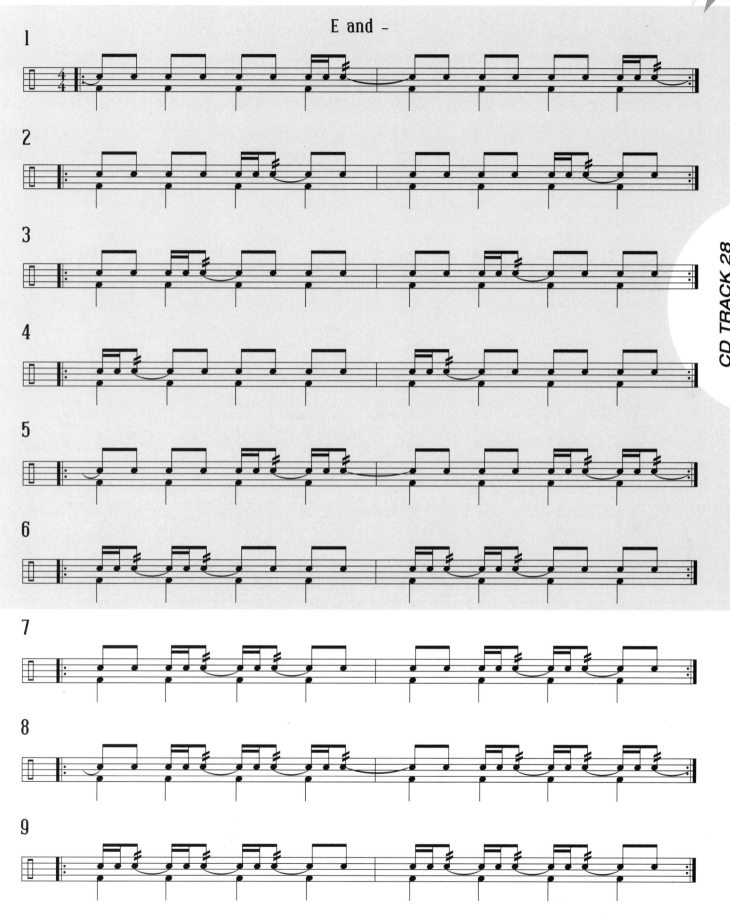

E and –

10

11

12

Twelve Bar Solo

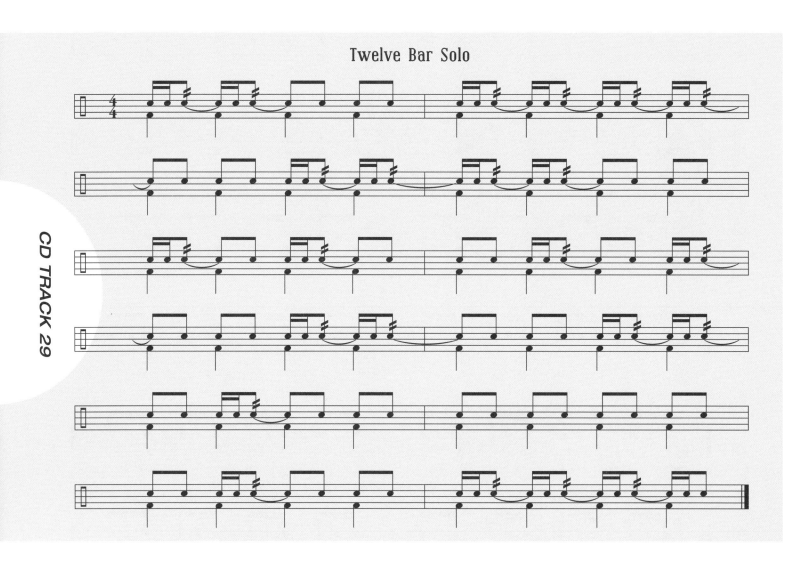

Rolled Eighth & Sixteenth Note Combinations

And A –

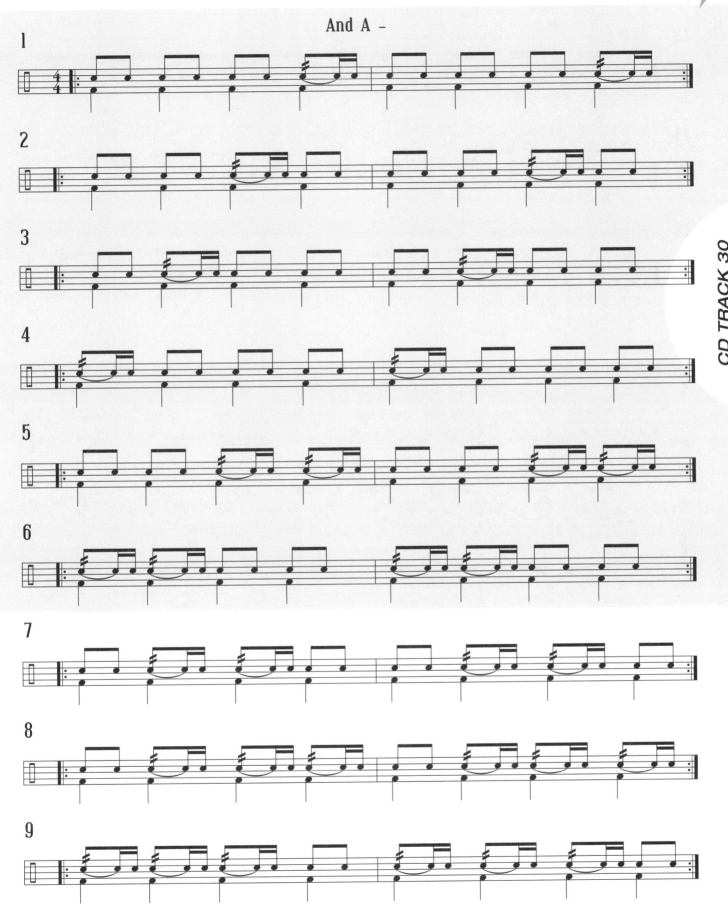

CD TRACK 30

Rolled Eighth & Sixteenth Note Combinations

E and –

10

11

12

Twelve Bar Solo

Five and Nine Solo #2

CD TRACK 32

Five and Nine Solo #3

Rockin' Poppin' **1**
Snare Drum

Quarter Notes & Triplets

CD TRACK 33

Quarter Notes & Triplets

Twelve Bar Solo

Eighth Notes & Triplets

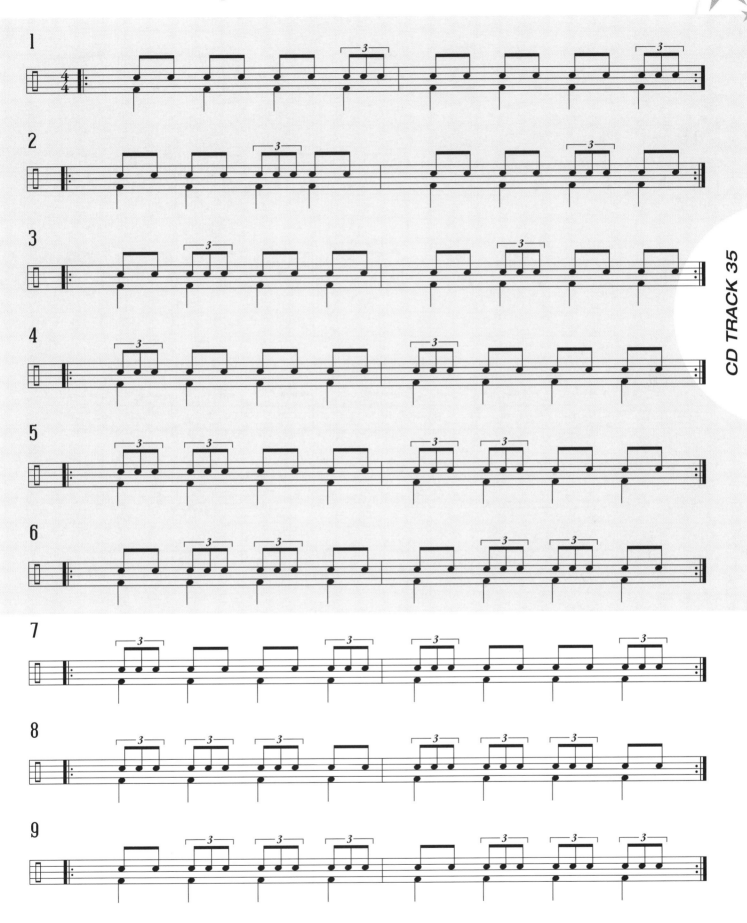

Eighth Notes & Triplets

10

11

12

Twelve Bar Solo

CD TRACK 36

Rockin' Poppin' 1
Snare Drum

Sixteenth Notes & Triplets

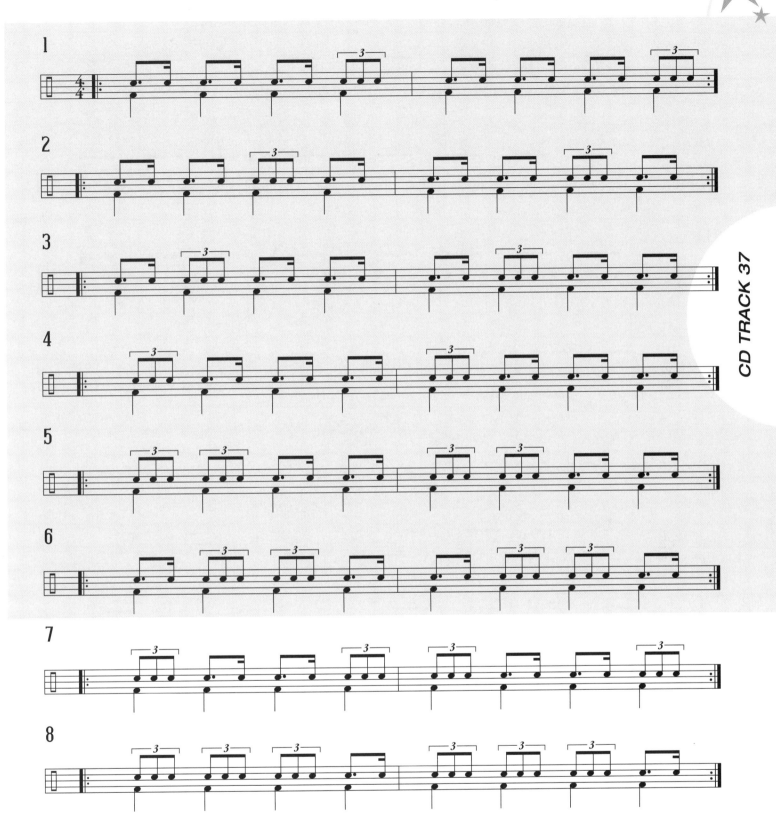

Sixteenth Notes & Triplets

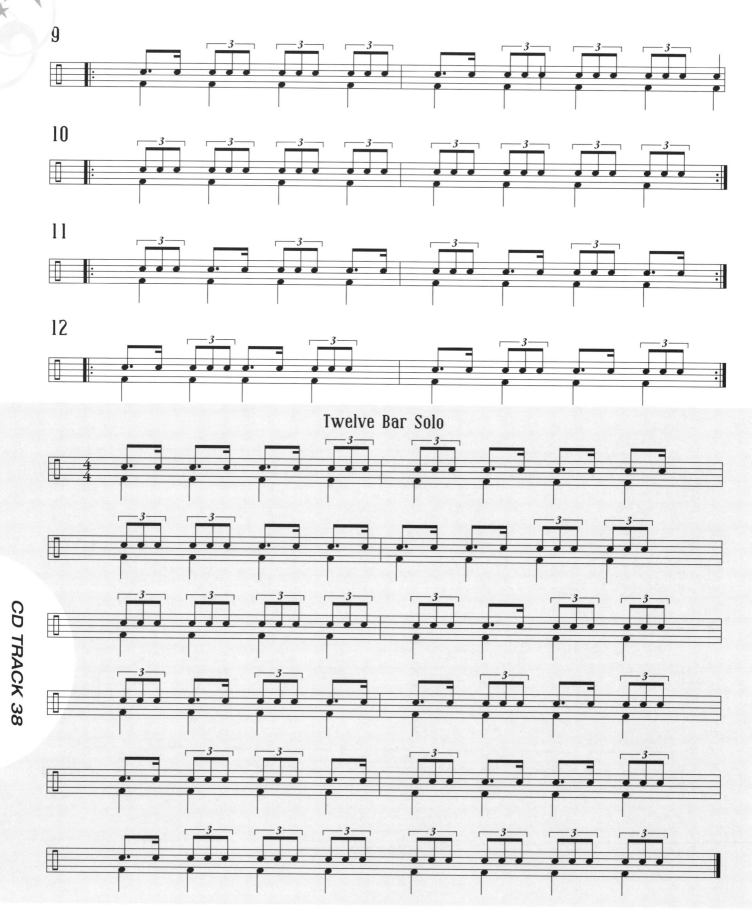

9

10

11

12

Twelve Bar Solo

Rockin' Poppin' **1**
Snare Drum

Triplet Solo #1

Thirty Two Bar Solo

Triplet Solo #2

Thirty Two Bar Solo

Triplet Solo #3

Thirty Two Bar Solo

Rockin' Poppin' **1**
SnareDrum

About the Author

Bart started playing the drums at the age of five and, has built his career on hard work and determination. Having studied with some of the world's greatest drummers, Bart has made a reputation for himself as a hardworking, solid rock drummer. Bart has provided the foundation for *The Sam Morrison Band* for over a decade. In his time with Morrison, Bart has been featured on five studio CD's which have to date, sold close to 200,000 digital downloads. They continue to tour worldwide on a regular basis. For more information on S.M.B. please visit *www.sammorrisonband.com*.

Bart lives with his wife Leah in Fullerton California where he is a highly sought after drum educator. He authored his first book, "The School of Hard Rocks" and went on to record an award winning DVD by the same title. He followed up his first book and DVD with a teaching aid entitled, "The Drummers Survival Guide", and has done two additional DVD's, "Drums ASAP, Set" and "Drums ASAP Rudimental Drumming." Bart is very active with all of his students' drumming endeavors helping out with talent shows and battles of the bands, when he can. He also regularly hosts master classes, summer drummer boot camps, and performs drum clinics. For more information on Bart please visit, *www.bartrobley.com*.